ROSA PARKS

BY ANNE SCHRAFF

Development: Kent Publishing Services, Inc.

Design and Production: Signature Design Group, Inc.

SADDLEBACK EDUCATIONAL PUBLISHING

Three Watson

Irvine, CA 92618-2767

Web site: www.sdlback.com

Photo Credits: pages 28, 37, Library of Congress; page 59, The Rosa Parks Library and Museum

ISBN-13: 978-1-59905-252-6

ISBN-10: 1-59905-252-0

eBook: 978-1-60291-613-5

Printed in China

12 11 10 09 08 9 8 7 6 5 4 3 2

TABLE of CONTENTS

CHAPTER 1

Rosa Parks, an African American **seamstress**, spent a hard day at her job in Montgomery, Alabama. It was almost Christmas. She had done some shopping. She headed for the bus. She was looking forward to sitting down.

But, as soon as Parks sat down, the bus driver told her to get up. He told her to give her seat to a white man.

It was the 1950s in America. Black people had to sit in the back seats of the bus. But, if a white person was standing, they were expected to give up those seats to the white person. Rosa Parks refused to get up. She was tired of being mistreated and **humiliated** just because of the color of her skin.

Park's refusal caused a major court battle. In the end, racial segregation on the buses was declared **unconstitutional**. Because of what the quiet seamstress had done, black Americans all over the South took a major step toward equality.

Rosa Parks' courage helped launch the civil rights revolution.

Rosa Louise McCauley was born on February 4, 1913, in Tuskegee, Alabama. Her mother, Leona, was a teacher. Her father, James, was a carpenter. Leona McCauley worked hard, cooking and cleaning. James McCauley traveled all around the state doing carpentry work.

When Leona McCauley was expecting her second child, she moved in with her husband's parents. The house was crowded. Leona was very unhappy.

One day, she packed up baby Rosa. She moved back to her own parents' house in Pine Level, Alabama. Rosa did not see her father again very much. She saw him once when she was a toddler. She saw him again as an adult.

Rosa's brother, Sylvester, was born at their grandparents' house. Rosa liked it there. She loved her grandparents.

When Rosa was about six-years-old, something frightening happened. Her grandfather was sitting by the front door with a shotgun across his knees. He told Rosa that the Ku Klux Klan was in the neighborhood. The Ku Klux Klan is a terrorist organization that attacks African Americans.

Rosa's grandfather said he would be ready if they tried to break in and harm his family. The Ku Klux Klan did not break in. But, Rosa felt sad that there were white people who would try to harm black people.

Rosa learned an important lesson from her grandfather. You have to stand up for your family and for your principles. When Rosa was older, she got a job picking cotton for fifty cents a day. Many black children in the area worked picking cotton.

Rosa worked from early morning to sundown. It was very hot, and the sun burned down on the children.

As she walked up and down the rows of cotton, she got big, red blisters on her feet. Since the blisters hurt so much, she moved up and down the rows of cotton on her knees. The children had to be very careful that they did not get blood from their blisters on the cotton.

At age nine, Rosa started school. There was a nice school for white children and a rundown school for black children. In Rosa's classroom, sixty children were crowded together. But even though it was difficult, Rosa liked to read stories and play games with the other children.

When Rosa was eleven, she went into a store for a soda. The clerk said black children could not sit at the counter and drink sodas. They could have ice cream cones instead. They had to eat them outside the store.

Rosa's mother had a great love for learning. She wanted Rosa to go to a good school. So, Rosa was sent away from her grandparents' farm to the big city of Montgomery, Alabama.

CHAPTER 2

Rosa Parks was enrolled at Montgomery Industrial School for girls. To help pay her tuition, Rosa cleaned two classrooms every day.

The school was in Centennial Hill in Montgomery. Like all public and private schools at the time, it was segregated by race. All the students were black but the teachers were white.

The school was started in 1866 by Miss Alice L. White. Miss White was a

Northern white woman who wanted to help the black people get educated after the Civil War.

Miss White was very strict, but she loved her students. They loved her back because they could see she wanted a better life for them.

Rosa learned a lot from Miss White. She learned a sense of pride. Rosa was a good student. She obeyed her teachers like she obeyed her mother at home.

It was exciting for eleven-year-old Rosa to live in a big city like Montgomery. For the first time in her life, Rosa heard African Americans **criticizing** segregation.

Rosa thought there was no way to stop segregation. But, she heard an exciting story of how some black people tried to end segregation twenty years earlier.

In 1900, some black leaders in Montgomery were very upset about how black **trolley** riders were forced to sit in the back of the trolleys. So, they told black riders to stop using them.

The African Americans in Montgomery did not use the trolleys for five weeks. They white owners said they could sit anywhere they wanted if they would only come back. The trolley owners were losing money.

So, for a little while, trolley segregation ended in Montgomery. But then, the white people brought it back. The black riders had to sit in the back again. This story made young Rosa think for the first time that maybe segregation would end one day.

Rosa Parks dreamed of being a teacher like her mother had been. But, when she was sixteen, she learned that her grandmother was very sick. So, she hurried back to Pine Level to help.

Then, Rosa's mother got sick. Rosa cared for her, too. The family needed money. Rosa returned to Montgomery and worked as a housekeeper. She was eighteen. It seemed her dream of becoming a teacher would not come true.

Rosa McCauley met a young man in Montgomery, Raymond Parks. Like Rosa, he was very religious. He was a member of Rosa's church.

Raymond Parks asked Rosa on a date. She agreed, mostly because he had a shiny, red car. But slowly, Rosa grew to admire Raymond. He did a lot of reading. She loved to talk to him. Raymond Parks was working on an important civil rights case.

A group of young black men were **accused** of a terrible crime in Scottsboro, Alabama. They were called the Scottsboro Boys. They were charged with attacking two white women.

The boys ranged in age from twelve to mid-twenties. They denied the charges. But, at the time in the South, the words of blacks did not count for much in court. The boys were convicted. All but the twelve-year-old were sentenced to death. The trial lasted only three days.

Raymond Parks and many other black people believed an **injustice** was being done to these boys. Parks held meetings and raised money to get the boys a new trial. Rosa McCauley admired his dedication to the cause.

It was dangerous for Parks to try to help the Scottsboro Boys. He could have been beaten or killed by angry white people. Rosa could see this man had a lot of courage.

Raymond Parks asked Rosa McCauley to marry him. She accepted his proposal. In 1932 they were married. Rosa was nineteen-years-old, and Raymond was twenty-nine. Raymond Parks was a hard-working barber, as well as a civil rights crusader.

Raymond Parks and the other civil rights workers had a victory in the case of the Scottsboro Boys. The United States Supreme Court overturned the convictions. The Court said the young men did not have a fair trial.

Rosa and Raymond Parks did not have money for a honeymoon after their marriage. They moved into a rooming house.

Both members of the newly married couple continued to work. Rosa Parks also helped her husband assemble paperwork on the Scottsboro Boys case. Rosa Parks became more and more involved in the struggle for civil rights for black Americans.

One of the women who had accused the Scottsboro Boys now admitted it was a lie. Even so, the boys were tried again. They were again convicted and sentenced to death.

But, the Supreme Court overturned the second verdict too. The verdict was overturned because there were no African Americans on the jury.

Finally, a compromise was reached. The four youngest Scottsboro Boys were freed. The others were **paroled** after a year. One man, however, was in prison until 1950. Rosa and Raymond Parks had helped save the lives of innocent young men.

In 1932 Rosa Parks finally got her high school diploma. She worked as a nurse's assistant. She also sewed clothing for white women.

In 1941 she got a job as a secretary at Russell Field Flight School. This was a **federal** facility, so there was no segregation. Black and white employees worked and ate together.

Rosa Parks loved the freedom of being treated like everybody else. On buses that rode around the base, she could sit in any seat. But, when she left the federal land and boarded a Montgomery city bus, it was different. She had to sit in the back with the other black people.

Rosa's younger brother, Sylvester McCauley, was drafted in the United States Army. He was to help fight World War II. The military was segregated, so he served in an all black unit.

Rosa Parks' interest in civil rights was growing. She joined the National Association for the Advancement of Colored People (NAACP). She volunteered to work as a secretary for the local **chapter**. She wrote letters, arranged meetings, and took care of the office. She was very **efficient**.

In 1945 American soldiers began to return home from the War. Among them were the million black men who had served.

Sylvester McCauley had a fine war record. He helped carry many wounded **comrades** to safety in bloody battles. McCauley thought that when he got home to Montgomery he would be respected for his service to his country. But, returning black soldiers were mocked and sometimes attacked.

There were white people who wanted segregation to continue. They were afraid the returning black soldiers would demand equality. So, these white people treated the black veterans even worse than before the war.

McCauley was spat on by some white people in Montgomery. He could not find work. So, he took his wife and two children and moved out of the South. He went to Detroit, Michigan.

Things were not perfect for black people in Detroit, but there was no segregation. McCauley got a good job with the Chrysler Corporation.

Rosa Parks visited her brother in Detroit. She liked the sight of black and white people living together. But, she was homesick for Alabama. She returned to Montgomery. She decided she would work even harder with the NAACP to make Montgomery a fairer place for blacks.

Rosa Parks was invited to speak at a NAACP convention. She was nervous because she had not done that before. But, she did a good job. She became self-assured.

Rosa Parks got a job at Crittenden's Tailor Shop in Montgomery. She was an excellent seamstress. She altered men's suits. She made dresses. Parks also continued to work for the NAACP. She also taught Sunday school. Life was comfortable for them.

CHAPTER 4

On the city buses of Montgomery, Alabama, black riders always had to sit in the back of the bus.

Also, black riders were not treated with courtesy. Drivers often called adult African American women "girl" and adult men "boy." They did not treat them with the respect they showed other riders. Rosa Parks discussed this humiliating situation with her friends at the NAACP.

Seventy-five percent of the people riding the Montgomery bus system were black. Most whites had their own cars. So, the black riders were supporting the bus system. Yet, they were badly treated.

Parks wanted to do something about this. But, she was not sure what she could do. She did not know anything about organizing protests or boycotts.

Some friends of Rosa Parks paid for her to go to a workshop at Highlander Folk School. The school was in the Appalachian Mountains in Tennessee. There she could learn about working for change in society.

When Rosa Parks arrived at Highlander School, she was nervous. Most of the other people were white. Parks felt strange. But, soon she fit in very well.

The white people asked her about segregation in Alabama. They were very interested in the stories she told about her experience with the NAACP.

At Highlander School, something happened to Rosa Parks that had never happened before. She was eating food other people made. She had breakfast brought to her on a tray. Parks was forty-two-years-old. It was the first time anybody had waited on her.

After the workshop at Highlander School, Parks returned to Montgomery and her seamstress job. Raymond Parks was now in ill health. He could only work part time. That made it harder on Rosa.

In August 1955 Rosa Parks attended a NAACP meeting. There, she met Rev. Martin Luther King Jr. for the first time.

She was very inspired by him. He seemed strong and fearless. Rosa Parks had fresh hope that conditions might indeed change for black people in the American South.

During the summer of 1955, Rosa Parks continued to work hard and volunteer at the NAACP. She did not expect anything dramatic to happen to her. But, her life and the whole system of segregation was about to be shaken.

On a rainy evening on December 1, 1955, Rosa Parks left her seamstress job as usual. She headed home. She ached all over from the long hours she spent hunched over her work. Rosa Parks had bursitis, a problem that causes pain in the joints.

The first bus that came was too crowded. Parks did not want to stand on the ride home. So, while waiting for the next bus, she did some Christmas shopping.

When Parks returned to the bus stop, she put her money in the fare box. Then, she went down the aisle to a seat. All of the front seats were for white riders. The back seats were for black riders. But the seats in the middle were for anybody on a first come, first served basis.

Parks sat down in the middle section next to a black man. She was glad to be off her feet and heading home at last.

When the bus stopped at the next corner, some white passengers boarded. The entire front section for whites only filled up rapidly. Some of the white riders were standing.

The bus driver came down the middle aisle. The rule was that no white rider would have to stand, even if that meant that black people would have to give up their seats. The bus driver came to the row of seats where Rosa Parks was sitting.

There were four African Americans in that row: Parks, a black man, and two black women across the aisle.

The bus driver told them all to get up so that the white man could take one of the seats. It was not allowed for a white person to sit in a row also occupied by black people. Once the white man sat down, the entire row became a "white row."

The black man and the two black women got up as they were told to do. Rosa Parks refused to move.

CHAPTER 5

The bus driver told Rosa Parks to get up or he would have her arrested. She refused. The bus sat there until two white police officers arrived. The officers arrested Rosa Parks and took her to jail.

Parks was led up a narrow flight of stairs to her cell. It smelled bad in the jail. Everything was dirty. Parks was put in a cell with other women.

Rosa Parks was arrested and fingerprinted.

Parks asked if she could make a phone call. She wanted to tell her husband what had happened. He was expecting her home. The jailer refused to let her make a phone call until an hour had passed. Then, finally, Rosa Parks called and told her husband she was in jail.

Word had already spread through the black community that Rosa Parks had been arrested. People who knew her saw the police taking her off the bus. Now, Raymond Parks and some white and black friends came to the jail. They paid Rosa Parks' **bail** and took her home.

Soon there was a meeting of the NAACP. The leaders saw the arrest of Rosa Parks as a chance to end bus segregation in Montgomery and the entire nation.

First, the black people of Montgomery would boycott the bus system. Rosa Parks would then be convicted of breaking the segregation law. At that point, the NAACP would appeal.

They would take the case all the way to the United States Supreme Court. They were hoping the Court would declare segregation on public transportation unconstitutional.

Rosa Parks' elderly mother lived with her. Raymond Parks was not well. Rosa Parks supported her family. She was afraid she might be fired from her job. But even though she was worried, she agreed to help with the bus boycott.

To start the bus boycott, the black leaders in Montgomery turned to two young ministers. They were Reverend Ralph Abernathy and Reverend Martin Luther King Jr. There were meetings in the black churches of Montgomery to plan the boycott.

The bus boycott was set for December 5, 1955. No black man, woman, or child was to ride the buses that day.

Thousands of leaflets were printed and given throughout the black neighborhoods. People were told to find other ways to get to school or work. If they had to, they were told to walk wherever they had to go.

The weather was cold on the morning of December 5. Rosa Parks and the other black supporters of the boycott were fearful. They thought most black people would want to ride the buses.

Many had long trips to work. They had no way to ride to work in automobiles. Most blacks had no automobiles and did not know anyone who did. It would be a terrible hardship to walk for many miles and then put in a hard day's work.

But, on that Monday morning, the black people of Montgomery surprised everyone. They boycotted the buses. The buses were empty as they rolled through the streets. The boycott was a big success.

The leaders of the boycott were from the Montgomery Improvement Association (MIA). They decided to keep the boycott going until the city of Montgomery gave in to their demands.

The MIA demanded fair and **courteous** treatment for black riders. They also demanded black bus drivers on black routes. They insisted that seats should be given out on a first come, first served basis. Black people should not be expected to give up seats they already had to white newcomers.

The MIA made plans to help the boycotting riders. They set up fleets of taxicabs, which charged the same fare as the bus. The few black people who did own automobiles agreed to carpool. Many adults and children promised to keep on walking for as long as necessary.

Rosa Parks came to court and was convicted of breaking the bus segregation law. She was fined ten dollars. Rosa Parks appealed the sentence. The whole issue of bus segregation was now on its way to the U.S. Supreme Court.

CHAPTER 6

In January 1956 Rosa Parks lost her job. She was fired. She did not think it was because of the bus boycott. But, it was very hard for the family.

Parks took part time sewing jobs to keep food on the table. Parks spent a lot of time doing volunteer work for the MIA. She found ways for many black people to get to work without using the bus. She coordinated rides for people. She helped set up special bus stops for black taxicabs at black churches.

As the boycott continued, the white business community was suffering. Black people did not shop in downtown Montgomery anymore.

The bus companies were desperate with all of their black riders gone. Some white people became angry. They made threats against Rosa and others.

On January 30, somebody planted a bomb at Rev. Martin Luther King's house. His wife and baby were inside the house. If they had not been in the back of the house, they might have been hurt or killed.

Some white people blamed King for making the bus boycott more effective. In February, Parks, King, and 86 other civil rights activists were arrested for setting up the bus boycott. There was an Alabama state law against boycotts.

Rosa Parks was becoming world famous now. News reporters came from all over the world to see what was happening in Montgomery. It was all because Rosa Parks refused to give up her seat to a white man on that bus.

Many people praised Parks for her courage. But, life was very hard for Parks and her family. Leona McCauley, Rosa's mother, was very ill. Raymond Parks was nervous and sick. He could not work.

All the pressure was having an effect on the family. Rosa Parks had no steady job. She found it hard to pay her bills. For the first time in her life, Parks took money from her friends to keep going.

On June 5, 1956, the federal court ruled that Alabama's bus segregation law was unconstitutional. They said it violated the Fourteenth Amendment, which gave equal protection to all Americans.

Alabama appealed to the United States Supreme Court. In November the Supreme Court agreed that bus segregation was unconstitutional. That meant all buses all over the South had to be integrated. Black people could no longer be told they had to sit in certain seats.

The bus boycott was over. The civil rights workers had won. Rosa Parks had won.

In December Rosa Parks got on a Montgomery city bus. She sat where she wanted. Nobody said a word.

The integration of Montgomery's bus system went well overall. But, there were some ugly incidents. Somebody fired a

Rosa Parks seated on a Montgomery City bus.

shotgun blast at Rev. Martin Luther King Jr.'s front door. Fortunately, nobody was hurt.

A sniper shot a black bus rider in the leg. Several black churches were bombed. But, nobody was hurt. Little by little, the white people of Montgomery accepted what had happened. All charges against Rosa Parks and her friends were dropped.

Rosa Parks had helped win a great victory for the black people of the

American South. But, she continued to get threats. People called her home and warned her to get out of Montgomery. Parks loved Montgomery. She did not want to leave.

Parks' husband was so upset. He seemed to have a nervous breakdown. Parks' mother was suffering too. Rosa Parks decided she could no longer ask her family to pay such a high price.

The Parks family was also suffering financially. Rosa Parks could not get a job anymore. Everybody knew who she was. White employers feared trouble if they hired her. There were very few black employers in Montgomery.

Rosa Parks sadly packed up her few possessions. They headed to the only place where they had family, Detroit, Michigan.

CHAPTER 7

Sylvester McCauley, Rosa Parks' brother, owned a large house in Detroit. He and his wife, Daisy, had thirteen children. When Rosa Parks arrived in Detroit, her brother helped her get settled. Rosa Parks joined the local NAACP. She looked for work.

Rosa Parks was offered a job in Virginia. She hoped to work in Detroit, but she needed to bring in money. So, she left her husband and mother in

Detroit. She worked for the Hampton Institute in Virginia as a hostess in the guest residence.

Parks worked at the Hampton Institute for a year. Then, she came back to Detroit and got a job at a small shop as a seamstress. She worked ten hours a day at the sewing machine making aprons and skirts. It was hard work, but now Parks could support her family.

While working at the shop, Parks met a black teenager, Elaine Eason. The young woman was impressed with Rosa Parks. She had read about her in the newspapers. She could not believe Parks was a seamstress in Detroit.

Elaine Eason asked Rosa Parks all about the Montgomery bus boycott and what it was like. Eason felt like she was talking to a celebrity. From then on, Rosa Parks and Elaine Eason (who became Elaine Eason Steele) were good friends.

Parks continued to be involved in civil rights activities. In August 1963 Rev. Martin Luther King Jr. led a large march for justice on Washington, D.C. Parks was there.

Then, in early 1964, Rosa Parks heard about a young black man trying to get elected to the House of Representatives from Michigan. Thirty-five-year-old John Conyers, Jr. was a lawyer. He was also a hardworking friend of civil rights causes. But, Conyers was not well-known. He would have a difficult time getting elected.

Rosa Parks thought John Conyers Jr. was just what the people needed in that district. She decided to help him get elected. She called Martin Luther King Jr. and asked him to come to Michigan to speak for Conyers.

King never made political speeches for people. But, he was convinced by Parks that he should make this speech. He came to Michigan and asked voters to elect Conyers. It was just what the Conyers' campaign needed. John Conyers, Jr. won the election.

When he joined the House of Representatives, John Conyers asked Rosa Parks to join the staff in his Michigan office. Some of Conyers' friends thought this was not a good idea. Parks was **controversial**. She had been in the middle of that bus boycott in Alabama.

But, Parks took the job and turned out to be an excellent congressional assistant. When people brought problems to Congressman Conyers' office, Rosa Parks handled them. She brought important issues to Conyers' attention. Parks was courteous and efficient.

Some white people in Michigan knew about Rosa Parks' past in ending bus segregation in Alabama. Some of them sent her hate mail. The letters **ridiculed** Parks. But, none of this bothered Rosa Parks. She had been through too much already to let hate mail get her down.

Rosa Parks became a member of St. Matthews American Methodist Episcopalian (AME) church in Detroit. She was made a **deaconess**.

In her job, she reached out to the sick and needy of the church and tried to help them. She visited church members in nursing homes and hospitals and prison.

Sometimes people would come to the church just to see her rushing around doing her work. They remembered seeing her picture in all the papers during the Montgomery bus boycott. Now here she was, quietly working in her church to help the needy.

Rosa Parks never took credit for having done anything outstanding. She just did what had to be done and remained a **humble** person. She knew she was well known because of the Montgomery bus boycott. But, she did not care about that.

CHAPTER 8

In March 1965 a group of African Americans marched from Selma to Montgomery, Alabama. Black people were being denied the right to vote in some places in the South. The marchers called attention to this.

Rosa Parks was watching the march on television from her home in Detroit. Suddenly, something terrible happened. White Alabama state troopers attacked the marchers with clubs. Men and women were knocked to the ground.

The marchers ran to a church and hoped they would be safe there. But, the troopers followed them into the church. They threw one man right through a stained glass window.

Rosa Parks was horrified. She had taken part in demonstrations. But, nobody had ever treated her like these marchers were treated.

Martin Luther King Jr. called Parks and asked her to come to Alabama. He wanted her to join him in another march. Parks had no money for the plane ticket. But, her brother's trade union paid for her ticket. She was off to Alabama.

King led the march this time. The Alabama state troopers watched. But, this time they did not attack the marchers. Rosa Parks was happy to have taken part in this march.

In 1967 there were race riots in Detroit. Rosa Parks spoke out against the violence. She understood that the young men were frustrated and angry. But, what they had done did not help themselves or others. They burned businesses. Rosa Parks' husband was working at a barbershop at the time. He lost all of his tools in the fires.

On the night of April 4, 1968, Rosa Parks and her mother were watching television. A bulletin flashed on the screen. Martin Luther King Jr. had been assassinated.

Parks and her mother wept at the news. King had done so much to advance the cause of civil rights. Now, he had been shot down and killed. Rosa Parks was filled with deep sadness.

Rosa Parks was now suffering from health problems. She had stomach ulcers and heart trouble. In the 1970s,Parks fell down twice, breaking bones. She still worked for Congressman Conyers. She was supporting her mother and, most of the time, her husband too. She had to keep going no matter how she felt.

For five years Raymond Parks suffered from throat cancer. Rosa Parks worried and kept hoping he would recover. She loved and respected her husband.

Raymond Parks was not perfect, but he had many good qualities. He did not mind that Rosa Parks' mother lived with the family. He never complained about having his mother-in-law in the home.

Raymond Parks was often very worried about his wife's participation in civil rights causes. He was so nervous that he sometimes could not sleep at night. But, he knew how much this work meant to Rosa Parks. He never asked her to give it up.

In 1977 Raymond Parks died. Rosa Parks was grief stricken. All through their marriage, Raymond Parks was often out of work and sick. But, the fact that he was always there giving his wife moral support meant so much to Rosa Parks. Now that he was gone, she **mourned** for him deeply.

A few months after Raymond Parks died, Rosa Parks suffered another terrible personal blow. Her brother, Sylvester McCauley, also died. When they were children, Rosa Parks always took care of him. Now, he too was gone.

At this time Leona McCauley was also under treatment for cancer. Parks was working full time for Congressman Conyers. It was a very hard time in Rosa Parks' life.

CHAPTER 9

Rosa Parks managed to care for her mother for two years while working full time. In 1979, ninety-one-year-old Leona McCauley died. Rosa Parks was nearing seventy. Now, she was all alone.

In 1979 Rosa Parks was given an award called the Spingarn Medal by the NAACP for her civil rights work. She also won the Martin Luther King Jr. Nonviolent Peace Prize.

She kept on working and overcoming her loneliness. Then, her friendship with Elaine Steel grew more important. The teenager she had met years before at the sewing machines was now like a daughter.

Elaine Steele helped Parks realize she would soon have to retire. Parks needed to develop new interests. At Steele's urging, Parks attended aerobics classes and studied **holistic health**.

The project that was most important to Rosa Parks now was the Rosa and Raymond Parks Institute for Self Development. Students at the Institute were urged to develop to their full potential. A program called Pathways to Freedom took students on tours around the United States.

Rosa Parks and Elaine Steele took a group of students to see the place where the Selma to Montgomery March took place. They also visited sites along the Underground Railroad. These sites were safe houses where fleeing slaves hid out. During the times of slavery, they hid while on their way to freedom in Canada.

Parks wanted these young people to know their **heritage**. She wanted them to understand the sacrifices black people made before them. These sacrifices were made so that they could have more equality in their lives.

Thousands of young people from all over the United States took these Pathways to Freedom tours in the 1980s.

In 1988 at age seventy-four, Rosa Parks retired from Congressman Conyers' office. Her eyesight was poor. She was growing very tired. She knew she could no longer give her job the energy it deserved.

Rosa Parks never did anything half way. She needed to give her all. But, her age was now catching up with her.

Rosa Parks was always interested in young people. She believed the job of the adult world was to show young people the way and to inspire them. She wanted to make the world a better place for the next generation.

To reach out to young people, Rosa Parks became an author. She wrote several books. The first book was titled *My Story*. It told how Rosa Parks refused to give up her seat on that bus. It was about how this led to the bus boycott and the end of bus segregation. She wrote in her own simple, direct way.

Rosa Parks wrote the book *Quiet Strength* to share her philosophy of life with youth. The book talked about the things that were very important to Parks. She wrote of her own religious faith and the values she held dear. She also wrote about the need to be determined to do your best.

For many years, children and young people wrote letters to Rosa Parks. Sometimes they were having problems in their own lives. They wanted her advice. Sometimes they were just curious about how Rosa Parks felt when she was sent to jail.

Parks gathered many of these letters. From them, she wrote her third book, *Dear Mrs. Parks.* She included the letters of the young people and her answers to them.

One young writer wanted to know why racism still continued to exist in the world. He could not understand why some people disliked others just because their skin was a different color.

Rosa Parks told the boy that everybody has to work together for a better world. She said that God created all people no matter what color they were.

For the first time in Rosa Parks' life, she had enough money to be comfortable. She had always struggled to make ends meet.

The **royalties** from her books, although not great, were enough to pay her bills. She even had a little left over. Rosa Parks was surprised to find that she had enough money that she did not have to worry anymore.

Rosa Parks never took a trip outside the United States until she was eighty years old. Then, she was invited to go to Japan and speak to the young people there. Rosa Parks was wondering if the youth of Japan really knew who she was.

When she arrived in Japan she was amazed to see eight thousand Japanese children lining the streets to greet her. They all were singing "We Shall Overcome," the famous civil rights hymn used in many of the marches.

When Parks returned to the United States, she spoke at schools all over the country. She enjoyed talking to children and hearing their hopes and dreams for the future. Rosa Parks lived in a Detroit apartment alone. One night a terrible thing happened.

She was getting ready for bed when a young black man broke into the apartment. The man asked Parks for money. She went to her purse to get him some money. Then, he began to hit her. He punched her in the face many times.

Parks tried to fight the man off. Finally, he knocked her down and took all of her money, about one hundred dollars.

Rosa Parks called Elaine Steele for help. She lived close by. She came over quickly. The police came and Parks was taken to the hospital. Luckily, she was not badly hurt. She said she did not hate the young man who had attacked her. She could not hate anybody.

After the attack, Rosa Parks moved to a more secure apartment. But, she did not go into **seclusion**. She kept on visiting schools and talking to young people. In one school in Philadelphia, the children chanted her name as she drove up. The children listened **attentively** to what she had to say.

In 1996 President Bill Clinton gave Rosa Parks the Medal of Freedom. In 1999 she received the Congressional Gold Medal.

President Clinton told the audience that when he was a little boy he had read in the newspaper about this brave woman. She was the woman who refused to give up her seat on a bus in Montgomery, Alabama. He said he was inspired by Rosa Parks' courage when he was a boy. Now, he was proud to honor her.

In December 2000 the Rosa Parks Library and Museum opened at Troy State University in Montgomery, Alabama. The museum is on the exact spot where Rosa Parks was arrested that day in 1955.

In 2002 a movie was made about Rosa Parks. It was called *Ride to Freedom: The Rosa Parks Story.*

The Rosa Parks Library and Museum in Montgomery, Alabama.

C H A P T E R 10

Rosa Parks was confined to a wheelchair in her later years. But, she continued to speak out on civil rights issues. She was an ordinary woman, a seamstress who never thought she would become famous.

Her act of courage and dignity that day in Montgomery changed history. For decades, black men and women had been forced to sit in the backs of the buses. They had to accept rudeness and humiliation throughout the South.

But one quiet, gentle woman took a chance. She risked her safety and her livelihood. For that, equality was advanced.

Rosa Parks died in 2005 at the age of ninety-two. She was a nonviolent revolutionary who made the United States a more just society. She did not do it for money or for fame. Neither of these had much meaning to her. She did it for the simple reason that it was the right thing to do. She did it to make the world a better place.

BIBLIOGRAPHY

Brinkley, Douglas. *Rosa Parks.* Thorndike, Maine: Thorndike Press, 2000.

Rosa Parks, Quiet Strength. Grand Rapids: Zondervan Publishing House, 1994.

GLOSSARY

accuse: to charge with fault or guilt

attentively: carefully

bail: money paid for the release of someone from jail

chapter: a branch or part of an organization

comrade: a person who shares one's activities or job; a friend

controversial: problematic; causing discussion or disagreement

courteous: polite

criticizing: putting down

deaconess: a female leader in a church; often a woman who works to help the poor

efficient: performing in the best possible way with the least waste of time

federal: having to do with the national government

heritage: background; ancestry

holistic health: an alternative to scientific medicine

humble: not self-promoting; modest

humiliate: to cause a person a painful loss of pride

injustice: an unjust or unfair act

mourn: to express sorrow or grief

parole: the release of a person from jail before the end of the sentence

ridicule: to put down or make fun of

royalties: a part of the money that is earned from the production of something that is given to the person who created it

seamstress: a woman who sews for a living

seclusion: in hiding; away from society

trolley: a car used for public transportation

unconstitutional: in violation of or not following the U.S. Constitution

INDEX